D0537240

Profiles of the Presidents

WARREN G. HARDING

★ ★ ★

Profiles of the Presidents

WARREN G. HARDING

by Barbara A. Somervill

Content Adviser: Melinda Gilpin, Site Manager, Harding Home, Marion, Ohio

Reading Adviser: Dr. Linda D. Labbo, Department of Reading Education, College of Education, The University of Georgia

COMPASS POINT BOOKS ✦ MINNEAPOLIS, MINNESOTA

Compass Point Books
3109 West 50th Street, #115
Minneapolis, MN 55410

Visit Compass Point Books on the Internet at *www.compasspointbooks.com*
or e-mail your request to *custserv@compasspointbooks.com*

Photographs ©: White House Collection, Courtesy White House Historical Association (59), cover, 3;
Bettmann/Corbis, 6, 10, 13 (bottom), 21, 31, 32, 38, 58; Corbis, 7, 9, 16, 28, 33, 47, 55 (left); Ohio
Historical Society, 11, 12, 14 (top), 15, 25 (bottom), 26, 46, 54 (left); Hulton/Archive by Getty Images,
13 (top), 23, 24, 27, 36, 37, 40, 41, 42, 50, 55 (bottom right), 56 (right, all), 57 (right, all), 59 (right);
From the Collections of Henry Ford Museum & Greenfield Village, 14 (bottom); North Wind Picture
Archives, 17, 22, 35, 57 (left); National First Ladies' Library, 18, 56 (left); Museum of the City of New
York/Corbis, 19; G.E. Kidder Smith/Corbis, 20; Library of Congress, 25 (top), 30, 44, 48, 49, 59 (left);
Stock Montage, 29; Union Pacific Museum Collection, 54 (right); Denver Public Library, Western History
Collection, 55 (top right).

Editors: E. Russell Primm, Emily J. Dolbear, Melissa McDaniel, and Catherine Neitge
Photo Researcher: Svetlana Zhurkina
Photo Selector: Linda S. Koutris
Designer/Page Production: The Design Lab/Les Tranby
Cartographer: XNR Productions, Inc.

Library of Congress Cataloging-in-Publication Data
Somervill, Barbara A.
    Warren G. Harding / by Barbara A. Somervill.
        p. cm. — (Profiles of the presidents)
Summary: A biography of the twenty-ninth president of the United States, discussing his personal life,
education, and political career.
Includes bibliographical references and index.
    ISBN 0-7565-0275-6 (alk. paper)
    1. Harding, Warren G. (Warren Gamaliel), 1865–1923—Juvenile literature. 2. Presidents—
United States—Biography—Juvenile literature. [1. Harding, Warren G. (Warren Gamaliel), 1865–1923.
2. Presidents.] I. Title. II. Series.
    E786.S66 2003
    973.91'4'092—dc21   2002153528

Table of Contents

★ ★ ★

A Front-Porch Campaign 6

Early Life 11

From Politician to President 20

Problems from Day One 28

A Struggling President 39

Scandal! 44

★

Glossary 51

Warren G. Harding's Life at a Glance 52

Warren G. Harding's Life and Times 54

Understanding Warren G. Harding and His Presidency 60

The U.S. Presidents 62

Index 63

*NOTE: In this book, words that are defined in the glossary are in **bold** the first time they appear in the text.*

A Front-Porch Campaign

* * *

Crowds gathered in front of the home of Warren G. Harding in Marion, Ohio. People arrived by train, car, and horse-drawn carriages. They came to hear this Republican

Warren G. Harding ▶ giving a speech from the front porch of his home in Marion, Ohio, in August 1920

◄ *Warren G. Harding and his wife, Florence, standing on the same front porch where he delivered campaign speeches in 1920*

candidate for president speak. During the months before the 1920 presidential election, about six hundred thousand people came to Marion to meet and listen to Harding.

A hush fell over the crowd as Harding stepped onto the porch. Harding was an impressive-looking man. He was tall, handsome, silver-haired, and smiling. He wore expensive suits and silk ties. His good looks drew people's attention.

Harding's talent as a speaker delighted and impressed his audiences. As a boy, he had enjoyed giving speeches in class. As a man, he improved his skills and could charm people with his smooth delivery.

When Harding became the Republican candidate for president, he decided not to travel around the country making speeches like the Democratic candidate, James Cox. Harding ran his campaign from home.

Harding spoke about helping the country "return to normalcy" after World War I (1914–1918), which had ended only two years earlier. Harding's speeches dealt with the United States and with patriotism. He wanted business to be strong and for Americans to prosper.

Harding's wife, Florence, had supported her husband throughout his earlier political career. Being first lady did not appeal to Florence. However, once Harding decided to run, she worked hard to get him elected president. She once said, "I have only one real hobby—my husband." Florence loved the excitement of the campaign. She later called it one of the best times of her life.

The Harding-Cox race was the first presidential campaign after the Nineteenth **Amendment** to the U.S. **Constitution** was passed. This amendment gave

women in the United States the right to vote. Women were pleased to finally have this right and took the campaign seriously. However, some people said that Harding would win because of his good looks and not because of his political skills.

▲ *Women in New York City casting their votes in the 1920 election*

Florence and Warren ▲
Harding looking over
election reports on
November 6, 1920

On the night of the election, Warren and Florence Harding stayed up waiting for a message to arrive with the election results. This was the first time election results were broadcast over the radio, but there was no radio coverage of the election in Marion. By 10:00 P.M., it was clear that Harding had won. The Hardings wanted to enjoy every moment of their victory. Little did they know how the pressures and demands of the presidency would affect their lives.

Early Life

★ ★ ★

Warren Harding was the first of nine children born to George and Phoebe Harding. He was born on November 2, 1865, in Corsica (now Blooming Grove), Ohio. His full name was quite a mouthful—Warren Gamaliel Bancroft Winnipeg Harding. His mother nicknamed him "Winnie," but he was usually called Warren.

Harding's parents had grown up on neighboring farms. They fell in love while at school. When the Civil War (1861–1865) between the Northern and Southern states began, George left to serve as a drummer in the

▼ *This photograph of Warren (middle) and two of his sisters was taken when he was six years old.*

Phoebe Harding ▲

Union army. Phoebe waited for George's return. They married as soon as he came back.

The Hardings moved to Caledonia, Ohio, in 1873. The family worked a small farm while George tried to build a practice as the village doctor. Phoebe ran the house and worked as a professional midwife delivering babies. Some of the Hardings' patients paid in cash. Others gave them chickens, eggs, or a side of bacon in return for their services.

George Harding was a born trader. He loved making deals. He often swapped horses with other traders and even became part owner of a newspaper, the *Argus*, as the result of a trade. Warren got his first taste of the publishing business working at the *Argus*. He worked as a printer's devil, which is an assistant learning the printing business.

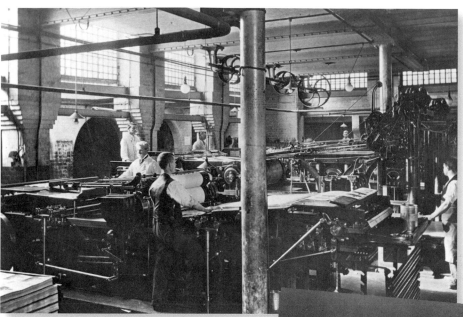

▲ *Printing presses in the late 1800s*

▼ *Harding, shown in 1920, enjoyed playing brass instruments like the tuba.*

The Harding children attended a local one-room schoolhouse. They learned reading, writing, mathematics, and a bit of geography. Warren also learned to play the cornet. Music was an important part of Harding's life. As an adult, he claimed to have played every brass instrument except the slide trombone and the E-flat cornet.

Young Warren had no interest in farming. His parents sent him to Ohio Central College at age sixteen. They hoped an education would help Warren find a career. The college had only three teachers and a few dozen students. At Ohio Central, Warren used his publishing experience to edit the college newspaper. He graduated in 1883, after spending only two years in college.

After spending only two years at college, Warren graduated at age eighteen.

The helicon is a type of tuba.

By that time, the Harding family had moved to Marion, Ohio. George was still trying to build a regular doctor's practice. Warren joined the family in Marion and started the Marion People's Band. Warren played the helicon, which is a type of tuba. Many cities and towns had their own bands during the late 1800s. Marion's band won first place in a state contest.

However, being in a band was not a career. For a time, Harding taught in a small country school near Marion. He did not like teaching, though, and he stayed only one term.

Harding also tried several other careers—law, selling insurance, and news reporting. Of these jobs, he liked reporting the best.

In 1884, Harding and two friends raised $300 and bought the *Marion Star.* The purchase included a building and printing equipment, but they were all in poor condition. During the next seven years, Harding worked hard to keep the newspaper going. He wrote articles and worked in the printing shop. He sold subscriptions to the *Star* for ten cents a week.

◀ *Harding at work in the printing shop of the* Marion Star

The offices of the ▲
Marion Star

Harding's easygoing manner set the tone of the *Marion Star.* The paper never took sides on any political issue. At that time, it was common among editors to speak out against politicians. Harding, on the other hand, never criticized or offended any group of people. His gentle approach to the news made the *Star* a favorite newspaper throughout Ohio.

To make more money, Harding gave political speeches and history lectures. He was part of a program called Chautauqua, which featured educational lectures and entertainment in a large tent. The Chautauqua group moved from town to town and charged admission fees for the programs. Harding often spoke in Chautauqua tents throughout Ohio. His favorite lecture honored his political hero Alexander Hamilton. One of the nation's Founding Fathers, Hamilton was the first U.S. secretary of the treasury.

▲ *Alexander Hamilton was often the subject of Harding's Chautauqua lectures.*

Back home in Marion, a divorced woman took an interest in Warren Harding. Her name was Florence Mabel Kling De Wolfe, and she was charmed by the handsome and friendly Harding. However, Florence's

Florence Mabel ▸
Kling De Wolfe
married Harding
despite her
father's wishes.

father was against the relationship. He even threatened Harding to make him leave his daughter alone. Despite these threats, Florence and Warren married in 1891. They moved into a new house, which remained their home for the rest of their lives.

Florence Harding worked at the *Star* with her husband. She had good business sense, and soon the paper was making a profit. Florence watched over every aspect of the newspaper business. It was her idea to begin home delivery of the newspaper. She even spanked the newsboys in front of the *Star* office when they misbehaved. Florence's contributions made the paper a financial success.

Their home life was not as successful. Harding had affairs with other women, including a ten-year relationship with Carrie Phillips, wife of a Marion businessman. Another Harding affair with Nan Britton may have produced a daughter in 1919.

◄ *A New York newsboy in the late 1900s*

From Politician to President

★ ★ ★

Ohio Republicans wanted Harding to run for office. They thought he had the perfect personality for a politician. He was pleasant, positive, and good-natured. He had no known political enemies, and he was already popular throughout Ohio because of his newspaper.

The state capitol ▶
in Columbus

As a politician, Harding (center) enjoyed greeting crowds and shaking hands

In 1899, Harding won a seat in the Ohio state senate. He served two terms before running for lieutenant governor of the state. He won this election, too. As lieutenant governor, Harding would take over if the governor died or left office.

Public life suited Harding. He liked shaking hands with people and once said, "I love to meet people. It is the most pleasant thing I do; it is really the only fun I have."

President William ▲
Howard Taft

In early 1906, Harding returned to Marion and his newspaper business. His term as lieutenant governor was over, and he didn't want to run for another office at that time. In 1910, Harding decided to run for governor, but he lost. This disappointment seemed to be the end of his political career. Harding appeared ready to permanently give up on politics.

However, things changed when he developed a friendship with President William Howard Taft. At the 1912 Republican **convention,** Harding gave a speech asking that Taft be the Republican candidate for president in that year's election. Although Taft lost the election to Woodrow Wilson, people remembered Harding's excellent speech. In 1914, Harding ran for the U.S. Senate and won.

During his single term as a senator, Harding introduced 132 **bills.** Most of these bills concerned minor issues, such as payments to **veterans** and loaning tents to the public to use as housing. As a U.S. senator, Harding also worked to get Spanish taught in public schools.

Harding's attendance record in the Senate was not good. He missed almost half of the roll call votes held during his term in office. However, he did vote for two important amendments to the U.S. Constitution. One gave women the right to vote. The other began Prohibition, which banned making or selling alcohol.

◄ *Before the Nineteenth Amendment was passed in 1920, women often participated in demonstrations to protest their lack of voting rights. Some, like these protesters shown outside the White House in 1917, were arrested.*

Famous baseball ▶
player George
Herman "Babe"
Ruth shaking hands
with Harding in
April 1923

In Washington, D.C., Harding became a popular golf partner, poker player, and baseball fan. He delighted in being a friend to all. His loyalty to friends was one of Harding's best qualities, but it later became his biggest problem. He trusted his friends without question.

At the 1920 Republican National Convention, three men were competing to become the Republican presidential candidate. They were General Leonard Wood, Illinois governor Frank Lowden, and California senator Hiram Johnson. The convention became a tug-of-war, with politicians pulling to get their favorite candidate chosen.

◄ *California senator Hiram Johnson was one of the candidates who hoped to win the presidential nomination at the 1920 Republican National Convention.*

▼ *Harding accepting his party's nomination to run in the presidential election of 1920*

None of these men had enough support to win the nomination. Finally, Harding's name was suggested. After ten separate votes at the convention, Harding won the nomination. According to newspaper editor William Allen White, "He was nominated because there was nothing against him, and [people] wanted to go home." The Republican candidate for vice president was Governor Calvin Coolidge of Massachusetts.

Harding campaigned for a "return to normalcy" from his front porch in Marion.

Harding stayed home in Marion, Ohio, and ran his campaign from his front porch. He spoke to large groups gathered in his yard about issues that affected Americans. The country was still recovering from World War I, which had been a brutal, destructive conflict. Harding's main issue was helping the country "return to normalcy." This phrase became his slogan. He hoped the United States could return to the way it had been before the war, but that was not possible.

Although the Harding campaign was run almost entirely from Ohio, Harding's message was carried throughout the country. His speeches and plans for the future appeared in newspapers and magazines. Harding's front-porch campaign was effective.

Harding won the November election by a landslide. He received more than 60 percent of the vote. The Democratic candidate, James Cox, received 34 percent. Two other candidates—Eugene V. Debs of the Socialist Party and P. P. Christensen of the Farmer-Labor Party—gained only a small amount of the popular vote. In the electoral college, Harding received 404 electoral votes to Cox's 127. Harding was the first U.S. president to enjoy such a huge victory.

◀ *President Harding delivering his inaugural address on March 4, 1921*

Problems from Day One

★ ★ ★

Harding needed to choose wise advisers to assist him during his presidency. He believed he needed expert help to deal with the major issues that faced the United States. Harding relied on his **cabinet** to help run the country.

Harding (left) and ▶
his cabinet

Some of Harding's cabinet choices were outstanding. Charles Evans Hughes became secretary of state. Harding knew nothing about international affairs, but Hughes was an expert in dealing with foreign countries. Hughes worked with Secretary of Commerce Herbert Hoover and Secretary of the Treasury Andrew Mellon to set up a foreign policy for the country.

Harding also appointed his friend William Howard Taft as chief justice of the Supreme Court. Taft was a former president, but he had always wanted to serve on the Supreme Court. Taft usually favored businesses over workers. He was against strong labor unions, which are groups of workers who band together to try to improve pay and working conditions.

Unfortunately, some Harding appointments were not so successful. Harding chose Harry M.

▼ *Former president William Howard Taft became chief justice of the Supreme Court in 1921.*

Daugherty, his closest political friend, as U.S. attorney general. Albert Fall, a senator from New Mexico, became secretary of the interior. Fall had been a friend of Harding's during his time in the Senate. Both of these men used their offices to get rich through illegal acts.

Other people who worked for Harding also used their government jobs for personal gain. These men included Charles Forbes, Charles Cramer, and Jesse Smith. Forbes and Cramer worked for the Veterans Bureau. Smith worked with Attorney General Daugherty. Harding died before much of their wrongdoing was discovered. He never knew how deeply these men had betrayed his trust.

Harding was elected president at a time when the United States was changing quickly.

Harry M. Daugherty became U.S. attorney general under Harding, but he proved to be a corrupt politician.

World War I had ended only two years earlier. The economy was failing. Many people were calling for limits on the numbers of **immigrants.** They wanted to restrict the number of people who moved to the United States from other countries.

The New York skyline is visible in the distance as immigrants wait at Ellis Island.

Prohibition began the year Harding was elected. As a result, people began making homemade "bathtub gin" and going to illegal bars called speakeasies. Selling alcohol became big business among criminals. Even Harding sometimes ignored Prohibition. When his friends came to the White House to play cards, Harding served beer and liquor.

People bought ▶
alcohol illegally
at speakeasies
like this one
during Prohibition.

Harding (second from left) riding to his inauguration in a car with (from left) President Woodrow Wilson, Speaker of the House Joseph Cannon, and Senator Philander Knox

Harding didn't stop having fun just because he was president. He held regular card games at the White House. He played golf every week. Harding loved cars and was the first president to ride to his **inauguration** in an automobile. He was also the first president to make a national radio broadcast and to keep a radio in the White House.

Florence Harding took her role as the nation's hostess seriously. Her parties filled the White House with laughter and music. She opened the White House to visitors and gave tea and garden parties. The couple chose not to have a traditional dance on the night Harding was sworn in as president. They thought it would be a waste of taxpayers' money. Instead, they opened the White House grounds to the public. The first lady said, "It's the people's house. If they want to look in, let them."

President Harding's workday often started at 8:00 A.M. and continued until midnight. Harding sometimes struggled as president. He said, "I am a man of limited talents from a small town. I don't seem to grasp that I am president."

The greatest problem Harding faced was the failing economy. During World War I, factories had worked around the clock to produce goods for the army and navy. War meant plenty of jobs, high wages, and big profits for factory owners.

Industries suffered from the war's end. Factories no longer produced war goods, such as ships, weapons, bullets, or uniforms. With no market for their goods, many factories closed.

The economy continued to weaken. To make more money, some businesses cut salaries and at the same time, increased work hours. Employees were often expected to work six to seven days a week and sometimes labored twelve to fourteen hours a day. In 1921, the New York Central Railroad cut wages for 43,000 workers. From January 1921 to the following July, more than 20,000 businesses closed and left 5.7 million people without jobs. Harding called on Secretary of Commerce Hoover to find a solution to the nation's economic troubles, but the problems were too great.

▾ *Grand Central Station in New York City*

During that time, the country was becoming more urban than rural. In earlier times, most Americans lived on farms or in small towns. By May 1921, however, more than half of the people in the nation lived in cities. Many new city dwellers were European immigrants. They flooded into Chicago, New York City, Boston, Philadelphia, and Baltimore. Many cities did not have enough housing, jobs, or schools to accommodate their growing populations. Many people had to live in crowded, dirty apartments called tenements.

Residents outside a ▶ New York City tenement in 1920

Many people did not want immigrants to continue pouring into the country. One of Harding's first acts as president was to sign the Johnson Immigrant Quota Act of 1921, also known as the Emergency Quota Act. This law limited the number of immigrants allowed into the United States. It was the country's first attempt to control immigration.

▲ *Immigrants being served lunch at Ellis Island while they await permission to enter the United States*

Harding struggled to find good solutions to problems facing the nation. Politicians and experts gave him advice, but it was hard to know what to do. He said, "I listen to one side and they seem right, and . . . I talk to the other side and they seem just as right! I can't make a damn thing out of this problem."

As Harding's first year as president came to an end, the outlook for the United States seemed bleak. The economy was stumbling, and more and more people were without jobs. European immigrants overwhelmed Northern cities, and Prohibition was creating countless legal problems.

Officials seize ▶ barrels of illegal wine in New York in 1921.

A Struggling President

★ ★ ★

During World War I, the United States sold war goods to European countries. Those countries were expected to pay for the goods later. After the war, the United States loaned those same countries money to rebuild their cities and industries. By 1920, European nations owed the United States about $12 billion.

None of the countries could repay their loans. Harding had not been president when the loans were made, but he faced the challenge of trying to collect the money. He could not force the nations to pay what they owed. The United States lost billions of dollars.

The country's economic problems did not improve. Many farmers were struggling to keep their land. Harding supported higher **tariffs** because he thought they would help farmers. Tariffs make foreign goods more expensive.

A community cotton gin in Madison County, Alabama, in 1923

This makes people more likely to buy the less-expensive American goods. This time, however, tariffs did not help. From 1921 to 1923, banks took over more than three hundred thousand farms because farmers could not pay their loans.

Fewer jobs and a poor economy led to violence in the South. African-Americans returning from the war wanted better-paying jobs. They also wanted an end to **segregation** in the South. Under segregation, there were separate schools, waiting rooms, and even water fountains for blacks and whites. In 1922, Harding gave a

African-American soldiers wearing the French Croix de Guerre, the medal they were awarded for bravery in battle during World War I

speech in Birmingham, Alabama, calling for an end to segregation. He was the first American president to make such a speech.

Harding was also facing problems within his government. In April 1922, Wyoming senator John Kendrick heard rumors of a deal between Secretary of the Interior Albert Fall and two oil companies. Kendrick discovered that Fall had received money from the owner of the Mammoth Oil Company to allow drilling at Teapot Dome, Wyoming. Another secret deal allowed an oil company to

Albert Fall (left) ▶
shaking hands with
American oil
executive Edward
Deheny, who was
involved in the Elk
Hills deal

drill in Elk Hills, California. It would be almost two years before all the details of the Teapot Dome affair were made public.

Republicans in Congress expected Harding to sign every bill they sent him. Usually that's exactly what he did.

Some laws passed by Congress and signed by Harding did not help the general public. For example, Congress cut taxes and got rid of wartime price controls that had been put in place during World War I. In 1922, millionaires paid about one-third less in taxes than they had five years earlier. The end of price controls on certain goods allowed businesses to raise prices as high as they wanted. People with little money suffered from the price increases.

As 1923 began, a new business boom started. Harding became a hero again. His popularity did not last long, however. Rumors of scandal and **corruption** ran through the halls of government. Harding had given his friends in office the freedom to do their jobs. Instead, they had done great damage.

Scandal!

★ ★ ★

Harding once said, "I have no trouble with my enemies. But my damn friends. They're the ones that keep me walking the floor nights." In 1923, there was no denying that Harding's friends had done their worst. Whispers of scandal floated through Washington. The scandals quickly became national news.

President Harding shakes the hand of a World War I veteran in Washington, D.C.

The first scandal to break involved the Veterans Bureau. This government agency arranged for payments to retired soldiers and sailors. The bureau also built and ran hospitals for veterans. Harding's friend Charles Forbes led the Veterans Bureau. Forbes and his assis-

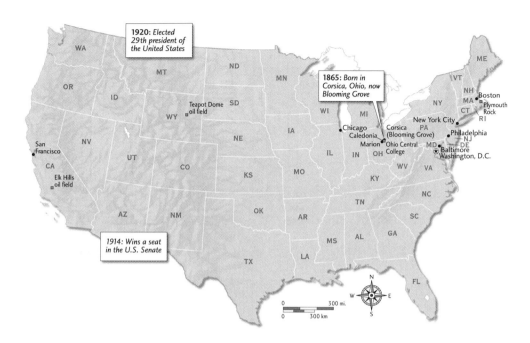

1920: Elected 29th president of the United States

1865: Born in Corsica, Ohio, now Blooming Grove

1914: Wins a seat in the U.S. Senate

tant, Charles Cramer, stole money from the agency. Cramer feared what would happen to him when he was discovered, and he killed himself in March 1923.

Forbes left his job at the Veterans Bureau. He was accused of stealing $200 million from the government. The money was supposed to have been used to build veterans' hospitals. Forbes was found guilty and sentenced to two years in prison.

At about the same time, it was discovered that lawyer Jesse Smith was involved in a **bribery** scandal with Attorney General Daugherty. The attorney general fired Smith and told him to leave the city. Ashamed of his actions, Smith also killed himself.

By June 1923, Warren Harding had had enough of the scandals. Florence had been in poor health for most of 1922. Harding himself suffered from high blood pressure and had gained weight. The Hardings decided it was a good time to tour the Western states and Alaska. They had always wanted to see Alaska, and had to cancel two previous trips there. Harding called this trip the "voyage of understanding." He hoped to regain voters' favor by making speeches and shaking hands.

President and Mrs. ▸ Harding shaking hands with admirers during their tour of the West in 1923

◀ *President Harding greeted children in Valdez, Alaska, during his "voyage of understanding." It was the first time a president visited Alaska.*

While traveling, Harding suffered from a bout of what doctors diagnosed as food poisoning, possibly from eating bad seafood. The Hardings checked into a hotel in San Francisco, California, to allow him to regain his health. On August 2, 1923, Florence sat reading to Warren, who was lying in bed. He suffered an apparent heart attack and died.

Even Harding's death became a source of gossip. Some people thought that Florence might have poisoned the president. They said she wanted to prevent her husband from getting caught up in the political scandals surrounding his presidency. There was no proof that this was true.

Harding's funeral ▶
train headed to
Washington, D.C.,
in August 1923.

Harding's body was sent back to Washington by train. After a ceremony in the Capitol, his funeral was held in Marion, Ohio. Florence Harding died the following year and was buried beside her husband.

Death did not stop people from talking about the Harding scandals. It did not matter to most people that Harding himself had done nothing wrong. His friends' acts of corruption continued to be spread across the front pages of American newspapers. People blamed Harding for being too trusting.

The details of the worst scandal, the Teapot Dome affair, were not revealed until after Harding's death, when Calvin Coolidge was president. The U.S. Senate had investigated the affair for almost two years. They discovered that Secretary of the Interior Albert Fall had received money to allow oil companies to drill on government land. Fall was tried and convicted of accepting bribes. He became the first cabinet secretary ever sent to prison. Fall served a year in jail and paid $100,000 in fines.

▾ *Albert Fall, (from left), Edward Doheny, and lawyers Frank Hogan and Mark Thompson outside a Washington, D.C., courthouse in October 1929*

Historians often list Harding as one of the five worst U.S. presidents. He admitted that the presidency was beyond his abilities. "I am not fit for this office," he said, "and should never have been here." Harding prided himself on being a great friend, yet he chose his own friends poorly. One of his biggest mistakes was failing to stop others—including his friends—from doing wrong.

This popular, friendly president left behind a legacy of scandal, greed, and corruption.

Harding was a loyal ▼ friend, but many believe he was a poor president.

GLOSSARY

★ ★ ★

amendment—a change made in a law or a legal document

bills—proposed laws

bribery—paying someone illegally to influence their opinions or actions

cabinet—a president's group of advisers who are the heads of government departments

candidate—someone running for office in an election

Constitution—the document stating the basic laws of the United States

convention—a large meeting during which a political party chooses its candidates

corruption—willingness to do things that are wrong or illegal

immigrants—people who move from one country to live permanently in another

inauguration—a president's swearing-in ceremony

segregation—keeping people of different races apart

tariffs—taxes placed on certain foreign goods entering a country

veterans—people who have served in the armed forces

WARREN G. HARDING'S LIFE AT A GLANCE

★ ★ ★

PERSONAL

Born: November 2, 1865

Birthplace: Corsica (now Blooming Grove), Ohio

Father's name: George Tryon Harding

Mother's name: Phoebe Dickerson Harding

Education: Graduated from Ohio Central College in 1883

Wife's name: Florence Mabel Kling De Wolfe (1860–1924)

Married: July 8, 1891

Children: Elizabeth Ann Christian (1919–), allegedly the daughter of Harding and Nan Britton

Died: August 2, 1923, in San Francisco, California

Buried: Marion, Ohio

PUBLIC

Occupation before presidency: Schoolteacher, newspaper reporter, editor, and publisher

Occupation after presidency: None

Military service: None

Other government positions: Member of the Ohio state senate; lieutenant governor of Ohio; United States senator

Political party: Republican

Vice president: Calvin Coolidge

Dates in office: March 4, 1921–August 2, 1923

Presidential opponent: James M. Cox (Democrat), 1920

Number of votes (Electoral College): 16,143,407 of 26,458,945 (404 of 531)

Writings: *Our Common Country* (1921)

Warren G. Harding's Cabinet

Secretary of state:
Charles Evans Hughes (1921–1923)

Secretary of commerce:
Herbert Hoover (1921–1923)

Secretary of the treasury:
Andrew Mellon (1921–1923)

Secretary of war:
John W. Weeks (1921–1923)

Attorney general:
Harry M. Daugherty (1921–1923)

Postmaster general:
William H. Hays (1921–1922)
Hubert Work (1922–1923)
Harry S. New (1923)

Secretary of the navy:
Edwin Denby (1921–1923)

Secretary of the interior:
Albert Fall (1921–1923)
Hubert Work (1923)

Secretary of agriculture:
Henry C. Wallace (1921–1923)

Secretary of labor:
James J. Davis (1921–1923)

WARREN G. HARDING'S LIFE AND TIMES

★ ★ ★

HARDING'S LIFE

November 2, Warren   1865
G. Harding is born
in Corsica, Ohio

WORLD EVENTS

1865   *Tristan and Isolde,* by
        German composer
        Richard Wagner, opens in
        Munich

        Lewis Carroll writes *Alice's
        Adventures in Wonderland*

1868   Louisa May Alcott
        publishes *Little Women*

1869   The periodic table of
        elements is invented

        The transcontinental
        railroad across the United
        States is completed (below)

HARDING'S LIFE

WORLD EVENTS

1870

1876   The Battle of the
Little Bighorn
is a victory for
Native Americans
defending their
homes in the
West against
General George
Custer (right)

1877   German inventor
Nikolaus A. Otto works
on what will become the
internal combustion
engine for automobiles

1879   Electric lights are invented

1880

Graduates from Ohio   1883
Central College

Buys the *Marion Star*   1884

1884   Mark Twain (above)
publishes *The Adventures
of Huckleberry Finn*

HARDING'S LIFE

Marries Florence Kling   1891
De Wolfe (above)

Wins a seat in the   1899
Ohio state senate

WORLD EVENTS

1886   Grover Cleveland dedicates the Statue of Liberty in New York

Bombing in Haymarket Square, Chicago, due to labor unrest (below)

1890

1891   The Roman Catholic Church publishes the encyclical *Rerum Novarum,* which supports the rights of labor

1893   Women gain voting privileges in New Zealand, the first country to take such a step

1896   The Olympic Games are held for the first time in recent history, in Athens, Greece (below)

HARDING'S LIFE

WORLD EVENTS

1900

1903   Brothers Orville
and Wilbur Wright
successfully fly a
powered airplane (below)

Becomes Ohio's   1904
lieutenant governor

1909   The National Association
for the Advancement of
Colored People (NAACP)
is founded

Runs for governor   1910   **1910**
of Ohio but loses

Gains national attention   1912
by giving a speech
nominating William
Howard Taft (above) for
president at the Republican
National Convention

1913   Henry Ford begins to
use standard assembly
lines to produce
automobiles (above)

HARDING'S LIFE

Elected to the   1914
U.S. Senate

Prohibition goes   1920   **1920**
into effect

WORLD EVENTS

1914   Archduke Francis
Ferdinand is assassinated,
launching World War I
(1914–1918)

1916   German-born physicist
Albert Einstein publishes
his general theory
of relativity

1919   Boston Red Sox player
Babe Ruth (above) hits
a record twenty-nine
home runs

1920   American women get the
right to vote

Presidential Election Results:		Popular Votes	Electoral Votes
1920	Warren G. Harding	16,143,407	404
	James M. Cox	9,130,328	127

HARDING'S LIFE			WORLD EVENTS
Signs the Johnson Immigrant Quota Act, which limits immigration	1921		
Becomes the first president to give a national radio broadcast Gives a speech in Birmingham, Alabama, calling for the end of segregation	1922	1922	James Joyce publishes *Ulysses* The tomb of Tutankhamen is discovered by British archaeologist Howard Carter
August 2, dies in San Francisco	1923	1923	French actress Sarah Bernhardt (below) dies

UNDERSTANDING WARREN G. HARDING AND HIS PRESIDENCY

★ ★ ★

IN THE LIBRARY

Joseph, Paul. *Warren G. Harding*. Minneapolis:
Checkerboard Library, 1999.

Souter, Gerry, and Janet Souter. *Warren G. Harding: Our Twenty-Ninth
President*. Chanhassen, Minn.: The Child's World, 2002.

Wade, Linda R. *Encyclopedia of Presidents: Warren G. Harding*.
Chicago: Children's Press, 1989.

ON THE WEB

The Friends of The Harding Home
http://www.hardingfriends.org
For online documents and links to other resources

The American President—Warren G. Harding
http://www.americanpresident.org/history/warrenharding
For a biography of Harding

The Internet Public Library—Warren G. Harding
http://www.ipl.org/ref/POTUS/wgharding.html
For information about Harding's presidency
and many links to other resources

The White House—Warren G. Harding
www.whitehouse.gov/history/presidents/wh29.html
For a brief biography of Harding

HARDING HISTORIC SITES
ACROSS THE COUNTRY

Warren G. Harding Tomb
Vernon Heights Boulevard and State Route 423
Marion, OH 43302
740/387-9630
To visit Harding's grave

Harding Home and Museum
380 Mount Vernon Avenue
Marion, OH 43302
740/387-9630
To see the house where Harding lived

THE U.S. PRESIDENTS
(Years in Office)

★ ★ ★

1. **George Washington**
   (March 4, 1789–March 3, 1797)
2. **John Adams**
   (March 4, 1797–March 3, 1801)
3. **Thomas Jefferson**
   (March 4, 1801–March 3, 1809)
4. **James Madison**
   (March 4, 1809–March 3, 1817)
5. **James Monroe**
   (March 4, 1817–March 3, 1825)
6. **John Quincy Adams**
   (March 4, 1825–March 3, 1829)
7. **Andrew Jackson**
   (March 4, 1829–March 3, 1837)
8. **Martin Van Buren**
   (March 4, 1837–March 3, 1841)
9. **William Henry Harrison**
   (March 6, 1841–April 4, 1841)
10. **John Tyler**
    (April 6, 1841–March 3, 1845)
11. **James K. Polk**
    (March 4, 1845–March 3, 1849)
12. **Zachary Taylor**
    (March 5, 1849–July 9, 1850)
13. **Millard Fillmore**
    (July 10, 1850–March 3, 1853)
14. **Franklin Pierce**
    (March 4, 1853–March 3, 1857)
15. **James Buchanan**
    (March 4, 1857–March 3, 1861)
16. **Abraham Lincoln**
    (March 4, 1861–April 15, 1865)
17. **Andrew Johnson**
    (April 15, 1865–March 3, 1869)

18. **Ulysses S. Grant**
    (March 4, 1869–March 3, 1877)
19. **Rutherford B. Hayes**
    (March 4, 1877–March 3, 1881)
20. **James Garfield**
    (March 4, 1881–Sept 19, 1881)
21. **Chester Arthur**
    (Sept 20, 1881–March 3, 1885)
22. **Grover Cleveland**
    (March 4, 1885–March 3, 1889)
23. **Benjamin Harrison**
    (March 4, 1889–March 3, 1893)
24. **Grover Cleveland**
    (March 4, 1893–March 3, 1897)
25. **William McKinley**
    (March 4, 1897–
    September 14, 1901)
26. **Theodore Roosevelt**
    (September 14, 1901–
    March 3, 1909)
27. **William Howard Taft**
    (March 4, 1909–March 3, 1913)
28. **Woodrow Wilson**
    (March 4, 1913–March 3, 1921)
29. **Warren G. Harding**
    (March 4, 1921–August 2, 1923)
30. **Calvin Coolidge**
    (August 3, 1923–March 3, 1929)
31. **Herbert Hoover**
    (March 4, 1929–March 3, 1933)
32. **Franklin D. Roosevelt**
    (March 4, 1933–April 12, 1945)

33. **Harry S. Truman**
    (April 12, 1945–
    January 20, 1953)
34. **Dwight D. Eisenhower**
    (January 20, 1953–
    January 20, 1961)
35. **John F. Kennedy**
    (January 20, 1961–
    November 22, 1963)
36. **Lyndon B. Johnson**
    (November 22, 1963–
    January 20, 1969)
37. **Richard M. Nixon**
    (January 20, 1969–
    August 9, 1974)
38. **Gerald R. Ford**
    (August 9, 1974–
    January 20, 1977)
39. **James Earl Carter**
    (January 20, 1977–
    January 20, 1981)
40. **Ronald Reagan**
    (January 20, 1981–
    January 20, 1989)
41. **George H. W. Bush**
    (January 20, 1989–
    January 20, 1993)
42. **William Jefferson Clinton**
    (January 20, 1993–
    January 20, 2001)
43. **George W. Bush**
    (January 20, 2001–)

INDEX

★ ★ ★

Argus newspaper, 12

"bathtub gin," 31
Blooming Grove, Ohio, 11

Caledonia, Ohio, 12
Cannon, Joseph, *33*
Chautauqua program, 17
Christensen, P. P., 27
Civil War, 11–12
Columbus, Ohio, *20*
Coolidge, Calvin, 25
Cox, James, 8, 27
Cramer, Charles, 30, 45

Daugherty, Harry M., 29–30, 45, *30*
De Wolfe, Florence Mabel Kling. *See*
    Harding, Florence.
Debs, Eugene V., 27
Doheny, Edward, *42, 49*

economy, 34–35, 38, 39, *40, 43*
Emergency Quota Act. *See* Johnson
    Immigrant Quota Act.

Fall, Albert, 30, 41, *42, 49, 49*
Farmer-Labor Party, 27
Forbes, Charles, 30, 44–45

Hamilton, Alexander, 17, *17*

Harding, Florence (wife), *7,* 8, *10,*
    17–19, *18,* 34, 46, *46,* 47, 48
Harding, George (father), 11–12
Harding, Phoebe (mother), 11, 12, *12*
Harding, Warren Gamaliel Bancroft
    Winnipeg, *6, 7, 10, 14, 21, 24,*
    25, 27, 28, 33, 44, 46, 50
  birth of, 11
  cabinet of, 28–30, *28*
  campaign for president, 6–7, *6,* 8,
    26–27, *26*
  childhood of, 8, *11*
  death of, 47, *48*
  education of, 13, 14
  inauguration of, 33, *33*
  lecture tours of, 17
  as lieutenant governor, 21
  marriage of, 18
  musical talent of, 13, *13,* 14
  as newspaper publisher, 15–16, *15,* 22
  nomination as presidential candi-
    date, 25
  as Ohio state senator, 21
  as president, 33, 34, 37–41, *42,* 43, 50
  as printer's devil, 12
  as U.S. senator, 22–23
  as teacher, 15
helicon, 14, *14*
Hogan, Frank, *49*
Hoover, Herbert, 29, 35

Index

Hughes, Charles Evans, 29

immigration, 31, *31,* 36–37, *37,* 38

Johnson, Hiram, 25, *25*
Johnson Immigration Quota Act, 37

Kendrick, John, 41
Knox, Philander, *33*

labor unions, 29
Lowden, Frank, 25

Mammoth Oil Company, 41
map, *45*
Marion, Ohio, 6, *6,* 14, 22, 26, *26,* 48
Marion People's Band, 14
Marion Star newspaper, 15, *15,* 16,
    19, *19,* 22
Mellon, Andrew, 29

New York Central Railroad, 35, *35*
Nineteenth Amendment, 8–9, *9,* 23, *23*

Ohio Central College, 14

price controls, 43

Prohibition, 23, 31–32, *32,* 38, *38*

Republican Party, 20, 24–25
Ruth, George Herman "Babe," *24*

segregation, 40
Smith, Jesse, 30, 45
Socialist Party, 27
speakeasies, 31, *32*

Taft, William Howard, 22, *22,* 29, *29*
tariffs, 39–40
Teapot Dome affair, 41–42, 49
tenements, *36*
Thompson, Mark, *49*

Veterans Bureau, 30, 44–45
voting rights, 8–9, *9,* 23, *23*
"voyage of understanding," 46–47, *46,*
    47

White, William Allen, 25
Wilson, Woodrow, 22, *33*
Wood, Leonard, 24
World War I, 8, 31, 34, 39, *41*

ABOUT THE AUTHOR

Barbara Somervill loves learning. She sees every writing project as a chance to learn new information or gain an understanding of a historic period. Barbara grew up in New York. She has also lived in Toronto, Canada; Canberra, Australia; California; and South Carolina. She is an avid reader and traveler, and enjoys movies and live theater.